D1415415

Argentina

Written by

Marion Morrison

Consultant Beatriz Casoy

Illustrated by

Ann Savage

SILVER BURDETT PRESS

ENGLEWOOD CLIFFS, NEW JERSEY

Series Editor Sue Seddon
U.S. Project Editor Nancy Furstinger
Designer Robert Mathias, Publishing Workshop
Photo-researcher Hugh Olliff

A TEMPLAR BOOK

Devised and produced by Templar Publishing Ltd
107 High Street, Dorking, Surrey RH4 1QA

Adapted and first published in the United States in 1989
by Silver Burdett Press, Englewood Cliffs, N.J.

Color separations by Positive Colour Ltd, Maldon, Essex
Printed by L.E.G.O., Vicenza, Italy

Library of Congress Cataloging-in-Publication Data

Morrison, Marion.
    Argentina / written by Marion Morrison; consultant Beatriz Casoy;
    illustrated by Ann Savage.
        p. cm. – (People & places)
    "A Templar book."
    Includes index.
    Summary: Text and illustrations introduce the geography, history,
people, and culture of the second largest country in South America.
    1. Argentina—Juvenile literature. [1. Argentina.] I. Savage, Ann, ill.
    II. Title   III. Series: People & places (Englewood Cliffs, N.J.)
    F2808.2.M66   1989
    982–dc19   88-29849
    ISBN 0-382-09793-9   CIP
                                                          AC

Contents

WHERE IN THE WORLD?

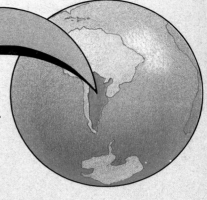

Argentina covers most of the southern part of the continent of South America. It is the second largest country in South America, after Brazil. Argentina extends 2,130 miles from north to south so its climate and landscape are very varied. The north is subtropical, while the far south is washed by icy seas from Antarctica. It shares its borders with five other countries: Brazil, Bolivia, Chile, Paraguay, and Uruguay. The Andes mountains stretch down its western border and to the east its Atlantic coastline is over 2,400 miles long.

There have been South American Indians living in Argentina for thousands of years. Europeans first visited Argentina in 1516 when Spanish sailors, looking for silver, gold, and other precious metals, sailed into a wide estuary to which they gave the name *Río de la Plata* (Plate River), or River of Silver. They called the land "Argentina" which means "silvery."

Argentina is known for its cattle-rearing and for its beef which is exported throughout the world. It also has world class soccer and polo teams.

The pampas
The pampas of Argentina are vast, fertile plains of grassland where thousands of cattle are raised. The pampas cover about 251,000 square miles – an area a little smaller than the state of Texas.

Patagonia
Patagonia is a large, dry plateau that covers most of southern Argentina from the Atlantic to the Andes. It is treeless but has scrub and coarse grass on which thousands of sheep graze.

Symbols of Argentina

The blue and white stripes of Argentina's flag represent the sky, and the snows of the Andes. A golden sun shines in the center.

The *gauchos* are Argentine cowboys. They are of Spanish and South American Indian descent. They spend most of their working life on horseback looking after thousands of cattle that roam the pampas. Gauchos often feature as heroes in the poems and songs of folklore.

6

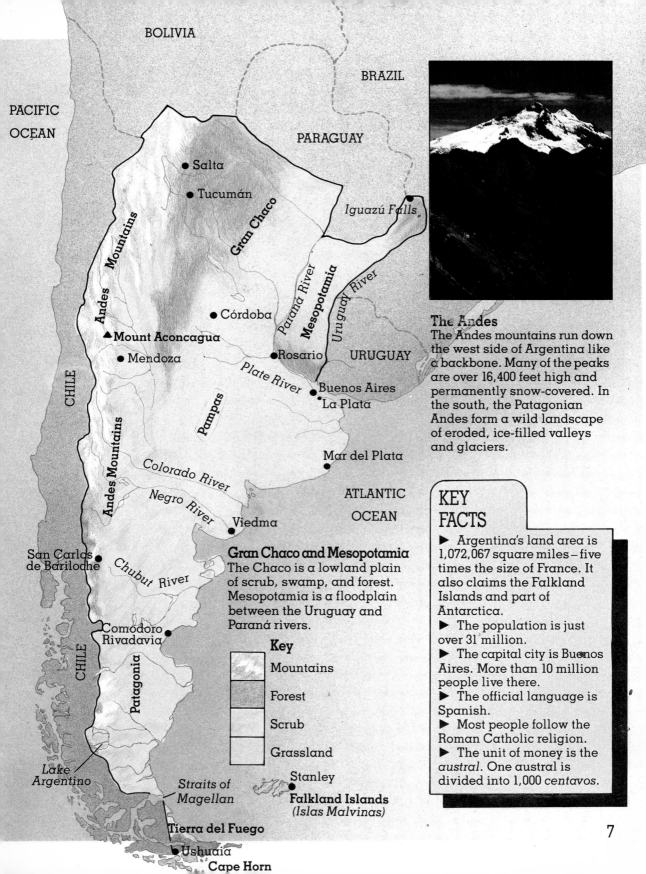

BOLIVIA

PACIFIC
OCEAN

BRAZIL

PARAGUAY

● Salta

● Tucumán

Iguazú Falls

Gran Chaco

Andes Mountains

● Córdoba

Paraná River

Uruguay River

Mesopotamia

▲ **Mount Aconcagua**

● Mendoza

● Rosario

URUGUAY

CHILE

Plate River

● Buenos Aires
● La Plata

Pampas

Colorado River

● Mar del Plata

Andes Mountains

Negro River

ATLANTIC

OCEAN

● Viedma

San Carlos
de Bariloche ●

Chubut River

Comodoro ●
Rivadavia

CHILE

Patagonia

*Lake
Argentino*

*Straits of
Magellan*

● Stanley

Tierra del Fuego

● Ushuaia
Cape Horn

The Andes
The Andes mountains run down the west side of Argentina like a backbone. Many of the peaks are over 16,400 feet high and permanently snow-covered. In the south, the Patagonian Andes form a wild landscape of eroded, ice-filled valleys and glaciers.

Gran Chaco and Mesopotamia
The Chaco is a lowland plain of scrub, swamp, and forest. Mesopotamia is a floodplain between the Uruguay and Paraná rivers.

Key
Mountains

Forest

Scrub

Grassland

Falkland Islands
(Islas Malvinas)

KEY FACTS
▶ Argentina's land area is 1,072,067 square miles – five times the size of France. It also claims the Falkland Islands and part of Antarctica.
▶ The population is just over 31 million.
▶ The capital city is Buenos Aires. More than 10 million people live there.
▶ The official language is Spanish.
▶ Most people follow the Roman Catholic religion.
▶ The unit of money is the *austral*. One austral is divided into 1,000 *centavos*.

7

WE ARE ARGENTINIANS

The early inhabitants of Argentina were groups of South American Indians. When the Spanish settled in Argentina nearly 500 years ago some married into the South American Indian groups. Their descendants are called *criollos*. By 1800, when the population was estimated to be less than half a million, the majority of the population were criollos, while about 30 percent were South American Indians.

Between 1857 and 1939 the population of Argentina changed. During that time about three and a half million immigrants arrived from Europe and Russia seeking a new life. Most of the newcomers were Italian and Spanish, but other nationalities included French, German, Austrian, Russian, British, and Swiss.

Most of today's Argentinians are descended from the European immigrants. Only about 2 percent of the population are criollos. They live mainly on the borders with Chile, Bolivia, and Paraguay. There are thought to be extremely few South American Indians left living in Argentina.

Although Spanish is the main language of Argentina, many other European languages are spoken and some South American Indian languages such as Guaraní are still used in the north.

Athletes
Argentinians have always been successful in sports. A world-record sum was paid for the soccer player Diego Maradona when he was traded to an Italian team. Gabriela Sabatini (below) is one of the best women tennis players in the world.

Welsh Patagonia
In 1865, 135 Welsh immigrants arrived in Patagonia. They had emigrated from Britain because they wanted to be free to preserve their religion and culture. South American Indians taught them how to hunt and so saved them from starving to death. Despite the hardships, they survived and later were joined by more Welsh settlers. Although the community has now mixed with neighboring Argentinians, the Welsh language is still spoken.

People of the port

People from Buenos Aires are called *porteños* which means "people of the port." The name dates from the time when Buenos Aires was the main port of Argentina.

Criollos

The *poncho* (cape) and skirt made by criollos from the northwest were once the typical clothes of the region. They are now made for sale to tourists.

9

FROM TROPICS TO SNOWS

As Argentina lies in the Southern Hemisphere, summer lasts from December to March, and winter from June to August. In the Chaco and Mesopotamia in the north, summer is very hot and wet, and often there is heavy flooding. Winters are often dry and mild. In the Andean region around Salta and Tucumán, in the west and northwest, there is very little rainfall, but melting snows from the Andes form streams that irrigate these dry foothills.

The pampas lie in the world's Temperate Zone where temperature and climate are not extreme. The eastern part is called the Humid Pampas because it has more rain than the western part which is the Dry Pampas. Sometimes violent wind storms erupt in the region of Buenos Aires, when cool winds from the south meet the warm air of the tropical north. These gales are called "*pamperos*" and are accompanied by heavy rainfall.

Despite its southerly position Patagonia has a relatively mild climate. The nearby oceans keep their warmth longer than the land and prevent Patagonia from always being extremely cold.

In the far south, there are spectacular glaciers. Tierra del Fuego, at the tip of the continent, has plenty of rain all year round.

Tierra del Fuego
The island at the tip of the continent is jointly owned by Argentina and Chile. Argentina owns the eastern side where the main town, Ushuaia, is. The island population is small and most of the people are sheep farmers.

Moreno Glacier

An arm of Lake Argentino in southern Patagonia is completely filled by the Moreno Glacier. The end of the glacier is a cliff of ice 197 feet thick and 3 miles wide.

Mountain forests

Forest covers the eastern slopes of the Andes in the provinces of Salta and Tucumán. The trees can be very tall. Heavy tropical rains fall in the region and it is humid and often foggy.

Plate River

Argentina's longest river is the Plate River. It is almost as long as the Mississippi. Water drains into it from an area of more than one and a half million square miles. This area includes all of Paraguay, east Bolivia, most of Uruguay, and a large part of Brazil. Here it runs through Buenos Aires.

11

WONDERFUL WILDLIFE

I ce and snow, mountains and plains, forests and swamps, Argentina's different habitats support a wide variety of wildlife. In the subtropical forests of the north live anteaters and tree-dwelling sloths. Sloths use their curved claws as hooks to hang upside down in the trees while they search for leaves and shoots, on which they feed.

The pampas are home to armadillos, the flightless rhea, and many species of colorful birds. Pumas, which are slightly smaller than leopards, live on the pampas and in the mountains, usually in remote, uninhabited places.

Llamas and their close relatives, the guanacos, thrive in the Andes mountains. In the far south, where the climate is cold, penguins and seals colonize the Atlantic shoreline.

Argentina has protected its wildlife and conserved its landscape by creating 19 national parks, and more are planned.

Darwin searches for clues
The naturalist Charles Darwin visited Argentina in 1833. He was sailing on the HMS *Beagle* as a member of a scientific expedition. His observations of the wildlife in South America, including giant animal fossils in Patagonia, led to his theory of evolution published in his book *The Origin of Species*.

The mara
The mara is a rodent and gnaws tough grasses for food. Maras are larger than rabbits and have long legs to escape from predators.

The armadillo
The three-banded armadillo eats insects and other small animals. When threatened it rolls itself into a tight ball, protected by armor-like scaly plates.

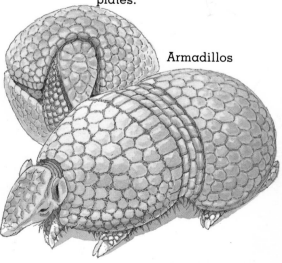

Armadillos

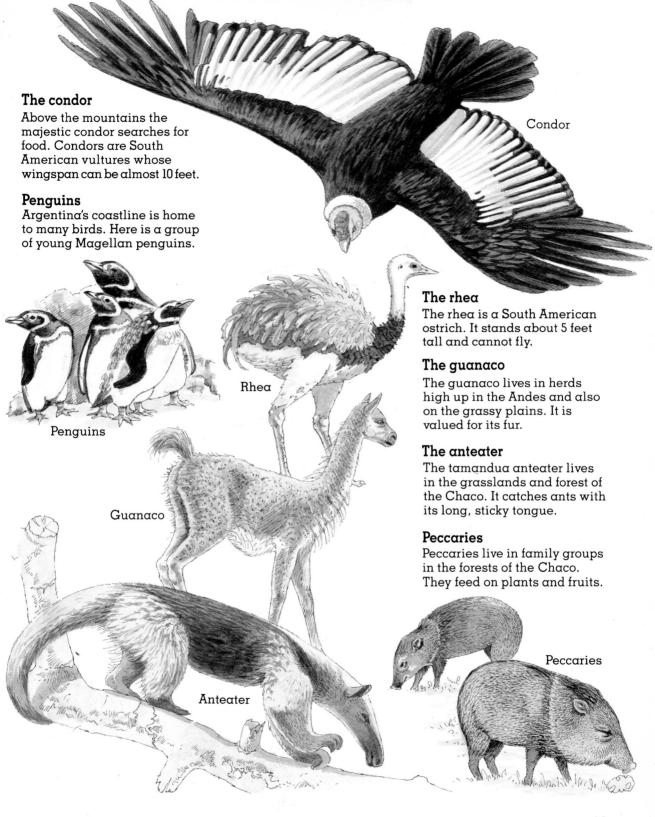

The condor

Above the mountains the majestic condor searches for food. Condors are South American vultures whose wingspan can be almost 10 feet.

Condor

Penguins

Argentina's coastline is home to many birds. Here is a group of young Magellan penguins.

Penguins

Rhea

The rhea

The rhea is a South American ostrich. It stands about 5 feet tall and cannot fly.

The guanaco

The guanaco lives in herds high up in the Andes and also on the grassy plains. It is valued for its fur.

The anteater

The tamandua anteater lives in the grasslands and forest of the Chaco. It catches ants with its long, sticky tongue.

Peccaries

Peccaries live in family groups in the forests of the Chaco. They feed on plants and fruits.

Guanaco

Anteater

Peccaries

13

A LAND OF PLENTY

The fertile plains of the pampas are the center of Argentina's agriculture. The area close to Buenos Aires produces vegetables, fruit, and milk. The southeast is home to huge herds of merino sheep and Aberdeen Angus cattle. Alfalfa and wheat are grown to the west, and around Rosario corn (maize) is an important crop.

In the 19th century the pampas were transformed from rough grassland. Good grass and alfalfa were introduced to fatten livestock, pedigree cattle were introduced from Great Britain, fencing was erected on large ranches (called *estancias*), and railroads were built to carry meat and produce. Refrigeration increased meat export to Europe. The livestock industry flourished.

Recently, Argentina has produced a greater variety of crops, particularly wheat, corn, and sorghum. Sugarcane, rice, citrus fruits, tea, and tobacco are grown around Salta and Tucumán in the foothills of the Andes.

A nice cup of tea
Yerba mate or "Paraguayan tea" is grown in the northern province of Misiones. Dried leaves of the yerba mate plant are ground to a powder which makes a refreshing drink when mixed with hot water. Argentinians drink from mate cups traditionally made of cow horn or gourds. They sip the tea through metal straws.

Land of sheep
Patagonia is one of the world's largest sheep-grazing regions. Sheep are also reared on the pampas. In the mid 1980s there were about 30 million sheep in Argentina. Sheep estancias in Patagonia are large. Some cover many thousands of square miles and are as big as Australian sheep stations.

Wheat on the pampas

Wheat is being harvested on the pampas. Wheat is the main crop grown in Argentina and increasing amounts of the pampas are being plowed up to grow it. Some wildlife, especially the pampas deer, are losing their habitat to the wheat fields.

Bringing in the catch

Argentina's fishing industry is not large but sea fish such as hake and anchovies are caught off the vacation resort of Mar del Plata. In other parts of Argentina river fish are caught. In northern Patagonia the dorado, a large freshwater fish of the salmon family, is popular.

Dorado

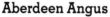

Aberdeen Angus

The Aberdeen Angus originally came from Scotland. These beef cattle adapt easily to different climates.

15

ARGENTINA'S INDUSTRY

For many years cattle and sheep provided Argentina with the raw materials for its main industries of meat canning and preparing skins and hides. Meat, including well-known brands of corned beef, hides and skins are still exported and Argentina is one of the world's leading wool producers.

Until recently most manufactured goods were imported but Argentina now produces much of its own machinery, chemicals, paper, steel, iron, and electrical equipment. Argentina has a shipbuilding industry and makes most of its own consumer goods, including cars, refrigerators, and television sets.

To support its industries, Argentina has developed its natural resources such as oil. Argentinian oilfields produce almost all the oil the country needs. The main oilfields are around Comodoro Rivadavia in Patagonia and in the Andean foothills near Mendoza. Since 1985 the government has been encouraging foreign companies to invest money to develop the oilfields further.

There are natural gas reserves in Patagonia, but until they are fully exploited, Argentina will import most of its gas from Bolivia. Several hydro-electric projects are planned, including the Yaciretá dam on the Paraná River.

Mining

Argentina has a wide variety of mineral deposits, most of them in the Andes. Minerals include copper, lead, tin, zinc, gold, silver, and uranium. The industry is not producing all the minerals it could. It is ready to be expanded. Here is a copper mine in the Andes.

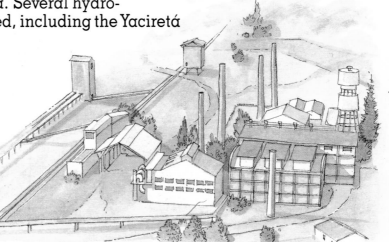

Leather

Leather goods are plentiful. Shoes, luggage, clothing, wallets, and purses are well styled and of high quality. There is an enormous variety of leather goods. Some are made from snake skin, and even the skin of the rhea is used. This is a leather shop in Buenos Aires.

Timber

Argentina has large forests and could produce more timber. Hardwood trees are the most valuable. There are many in the Chaco including the quebracho tree which provides an important ingredient used in the tanning process in the leather industry.

17

Argentina had a large railroad system before it had roads. The railroads were built to open up the pampa and British money and engineers were largely responsible for the construction. Between 1870 and 1891 the network increased from 457 miles of track to 7,755 miles. The railroad lines ran through the pampas to the ports on the coast, especially to Buenos Aires, but the rest of the country was poorly served. Today there are still no connections south of San Carlos de Bariloche and Esquel although there are international lines to all neighboring countries.

The railroads no longer carry much freight or passenger traffic. Most freight is transported by road. Highways cross the country and reach most remote parts but many of the roads are unpaved. Many people prefer to travel the long distances by air. Argentina has one international airline, Aerolíneas Argentinas, and two national companies, Austral and Lapa, as well as military airlines.

Catching a bus
Small buses called *colectivos* provide an efficient service in cities. Bus travel, even over long distances, is popular and comfortable.

Flying south
Air travel is very important in reaching remote regions. The Army airline LADE and the Navy have services to Patagonia that civilians may use.

Key
— Pan American Highway
+–+–+ Railroads
— Other main routes

International highway
The Pan American Highway runs down the west coast of South America. Four branches run from Buenos Aires to Chile, Bolivia, Paraguay, and Brazil.

Steam stations
Steam trains are often seen in parts of Argentina. Here, a steam train waits in Tucumán station.

Mountain hazards
Landslides are common in the Andes mountains and large bulldozers are used to keep the roads open. Traveling can be extremely difficult in the rainy seasons.

19

ARTS AND CULTURE

The arts in Argentina have been influenced by a mixture of several different cultures: first South American Indian, then Spanish, then other European cultures. All these have become woven together over the centuries to give Argentina its present-day culture.

Virtually no pure South American Indian culture survives in Argentina today because most of the Indian groups were destroyed in the last century. European influence led to the opening of many museums, libraries, and art galleries in Buenos Aires and other cities. At the end of the 19th century the French had a particularly strong influence in these areas.

By the beginning of the 20th century Argentinians wanted a cultural identity of their own. A nationalist movement began and Argentinian composers, writers, and artists were encouraged to produce works. The renowned composer Alberto Ginastera (1916-1983) was part of this movement as a young man.

Argentina has a thriving film industry. In the 1960s, under the influence of the "new cinema" of Latin America, films often had political and social themes. These themes were revived in the late 1980s.

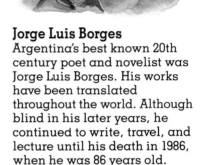

Jorge Luis Borges
Argentina's best known 20th century poet and novelist was Jorge Luis Borges. His works have been translated throughout the world. Although blind in his later years, he continued to write, travel, and lecture until his death in 1986, when he was 86 years old.

The tango
The tango is one of the best known of Latin American popular dances. The word "tango" probably came from the name of a drum used by black slaves. The music was made internationally famous by Carlos Gardel, a popular singer who came from an underprivileged district of Buenos Aires and died in 1935.

Colón Theatre

The Colón Theatre in Buenos Aires is one of the world's leading opera houses. It opened in 1908 with a performance of *Aida*. Many opera stars have performed there, including Enrico Caruso, Maria Callas, and Placido Domingo.

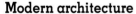

Modern architecture

The Lloyds Bank building is one of the outstanding modern buildings of Buenos Aires. It was designed by the architects Sánchez Elía, Peralta Ramos, Agostini, and Clorindo Testa and opened in 1966.

THE CITIES OF ARGENTINA

T he biggest city in Argentina is the capital, Buenos Aires. More than three million people live in the city itself and another seven million in the immediate, surrounding area. Buenos Aires means "good air." The Spanish settlers who founded the city may have given it this name because of the fresh breezes from the Plate River estuary on which the city stands.

Buenos Aires is sometimes known as the Paris of the Southern Hemisphere because it is a sophisticated and elegant city showing a strong European influence. Many of its late 19th century buildings copied French design. Some residential areas, such as Hurlingham where cricket and polo are played regularly, are particularly English in atmosphere.

One of the main avenues, the 9 de Julio, is among the widest in the world. The main shopping area around Calle Florida is closed to traffic. It is lined with shops, tea rooms, and restaurants and, because shops stay open late, it is filled with shoppers and sightseers most of the day and into the night.

Córdoba
Córdoba is Argentina's second largest city. Its population is about one million. It was founded by Spanish settlers in 1573 and has many fine buildings dating from that time. This was the viceroy's (governor's) house. It is now a museum.

"Cinema street"
Calle Lavalle in Buenos Aires has so many movie houses and theaters that it is often known as "cinema street." There are 250 movie houses and 70 theaters in the capital city.

22

Salta

This beautiful city was founded by the Spanish in 1582. Among its treasures is the decorated altar in the cathedral (right).

Main square

Plaza de Mayo (above), in Buenos Aires, has several important buildings, including the cathedral. All of one side is taken up with the presidential palace – the Casa Rosada. The memorial celebrating independence is at one end of the square.

Southernmost city

Ushuaia (right) is the world's most southerly city. It takes five hours to fly there from Buenos Aires and is Argentina's main city in Tierra del Fuego.

THE EARLY YEARS

The first inhabitants of Argentina, in about 10,000 BC, were South American Indians. There were several different groups. Some were hunters, fishermen, gatherers of nuts and fruits, others were farmers. Those with the most advanced way of life were the Indians living in the foothills of the Andes.

The tribes of Patagonia were hunters and fishermen. Some, like the Patagones and the Onas lived on the plains, others like the Yahgans lived along the rivers near the coast. Other hunting groups lived on the pampas and in the Chaco, including the fearsome Querandí or "eaters of grease," so called because there were fond of eating fats and blood.

The Guaraní who lived in the north near the Paraná river were fishermen and farmers. In their jungle home they grew corn (maize), sweet potatoes, and cassava, an edible root. They lived in thatched houses in villages and the women wove wild cotton into lengths of cloth for clothes.

The Andean Indians were also farmers. They cut terraces (level fields in steps) into the mountainsides on which they grew corn, beans, and potatoes. They relied on the domestic llama for wool and to carry their burdens across the mountains.

Big feet

The Patagones or Tehuelche Indians (below) were almost 6 feet tall and looked even bigger because they wore thick furs to keep warm. In 1520 Magellan's men named their land Patagonia or "land of the big feet" because the Indians' feet looked huge. In fact they stuffed their boots with grass to keep out the cold. They hunted the guanaco, a kind of llama, with a *bolas* – pieces of leather, weighted with stones, which when thrown, wound around the legs or body of the animal.

Mysterious Menhires

This group of granite stones, known as the Menhires, is in the desert hills behind Tucumán. It is thought that a South American Indian group placed them there about 2,000 years ago, but why they are there is a mystery.

The Mylodon Cave

In 1895 a German sea captain found some huge bones in a cave in Patagonia. Experts believe they are the remains of a giant ground sloth or mylodon (below) that lived about 9000 BC. Patagonian Indian legends suggest that their ancestors were familiar with these huge animals.

Fire watchers

The Yahgan Indians of Tierra del Fuego (above) helped to give the island its name. They always kept fires alight to keep warm. When European explorers sailed past the islands at night and saw the fires, they called the islands Tierra del Fuego which means "land of fire." The Yahgans amazed early explorers by wearing no clothes or wearing only a seal skin to protect themselves from icy winds.

THE COLONIAL YEARS

At the beginning of the 16th century the Spanish entered what is now Argentina from two directions. In the west Spanish soldiers crossed the Andes and founded towns that grew wealthy with the discovery of silver in the mountains. These included Tucumán, Córdoba, and Argentina's oldest town Santiago del Estero, founded in 1553. To the east, the Spanish explorer Juan de Solís sailed into the Plate River in 1516. Buenos Aires was founded in 1573.

The Spanish crown did not regard Argentina as an independent country. It was governed from Peru by a Spanish viceroy. Trade also was controlled by Peru and all goods had to pass through there even if they were going to Europe.

The western towns flourished for 200 years. Off to the east Buenos Aires was ignored and found trading difficult because of its location. The situation caused a rift between Buenos Aires and the rest of Argentina that still exists today.

Eventually Buenos Aires secretly began to trade directly with Europe. Their illegal trade was so successful that in 1776 Spain had to make Buenos Aires the capital of the region with freedom to trade. It was not long before the tradesmen of Buenos Aires demanded that all of Argentina be free from Spanish rule and the fight for independence began.

May 25, 1810
On this date the Buenos Aires *cabildo* or town council seized power from the Spanish viceroy (governor). This monument, in the Plaza de Mayo, commemorates the day.

Independence hero
General José de San Martin (left) led Argentina's fight for independence which took several years. Some bloody battles were fought but Argentina finally became an independent nation in 1816. Many towns in Argentina have a statue to their national hero.

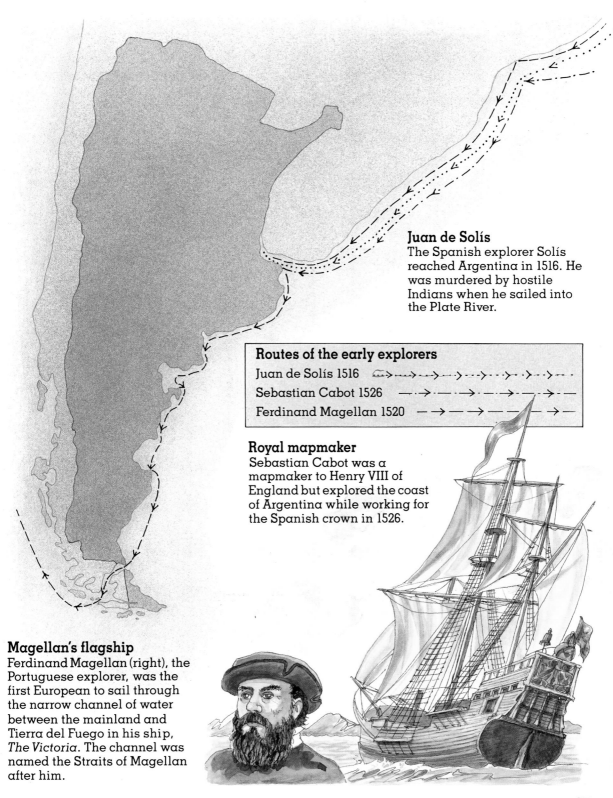

Juan de Solís
The Spanish explorer Solís reached Argentina in 1516. He was murdered by hostile Indians when he sailed into the Plate River.

Routes of the early explorers
Juan de Solís 1516	⌐⇢ ⇢ ⇢ ⇢ ⇢ ⇢ ⇢ ⇢
Sebastian Cabot 1526	— → — → — → — → —
Ferdinand Magellan 1520	— → — → — → — →

Royal mapmaker
Sebastian Cabot was a mapmaker to Henry VIII of England but explored the coast of Argentina while working for the Spanish crown in 1526.

Magellan's flagship
Ferdinand Magellan (right), the Portuguese explorer, was the first European to sail through the narrow channel of water between the mainland and Tierra del Fuego in his ship, *The Victoria*. The channel was named the Straits of Magellan after him.

A NEW NATION

Argentina gained independence in 1816 but the country's problems were not over. The division between Buenos Aires and the rest of the country continued. During most of the 19th century there was conflict between those who wanted Buenos Aires to be the center of government (the Unitarios) and those who did not (the Federales).

It was a period of unrest. There were frequent outbreaks of civil war, and the country had several presidents. Some were able leaders, such as Bartolomé Mitre who encouraged education and social reform. Others were not. The most unpopular was the dictator Juan Manuel de Rosas whose reign of terror lasted from 1829-1852. His band of red-robed assassins murdered his opponents.

In spite of the difficulties, many Argentinians became wealthy in the last years of the 19th century. Beef exports reached record levels helped by the building of railroads, the development of the pampas and the arrival of expert farmers from Europe. The small port of Buenos Aires grew into one of the great cities of the world.

Yahgans in England
In 1830 four Yahgan Indians from Tierra del Fuego arrived in England with Captain Fitzroy of the *Beagle* who called them Boat Memory, Fuegia Basket, Jemmy Button, and York Minster. Boat Memory died but the others survived and were presented to the king. They returned to Tierra del Fuego after a year.

Fuegia Basket

Jemmy Button

York Minster

28

The scholar president
General Bartolomé Mitre (left) was elected President of Argentina in 1862. He was a successful soldier, historian, and scholar. During his presidency he encouraged foreign trade, began to construct railroads, and built schools.

War of the Desert
Most of Argentina's Indians were destroyed during the 19th century. Many died of diseases brought from Europe, others were killed by settlers who moved into their territory. Some Patagonian Indians fought back. General Roca (right) was sent to crush them and they were defeated in the War of the Desert 1879-1880.

ARGENTINA IN THE 20th CENTURY

In 1916 Hipólito Yrigoyen, leader of the Radical party, became Argentina's first freely elected president. His presidency ended when a group of military officers seized power in 1930. Argentina has had several military coups this century. They usually have been followed by a period of military rule after which the country often returns to government by an elected president.

In 1946, after a period of military rule, General Juan Perón was elected president. Perón and his wife, Eva, worked hard to bring about social change: women were given the vote, and health care, education, and housing improved. However, Perón's social reforms were expensive and he was forced out of office in 1955.

Various presidents followed, but in 1976 there was another military coup. After it, Argentina was ruled by military officers who imprisoned and sometimes executed their opponents. They also led Argentina into conflict with Great Britain over ownership of the Falkland Islands. When this venture failed they fell from power. Civilian government returned in 1983 with the democratic election of President Raúl Alfonsín. Alfonsín faces a major problem with the economy. Argentina has borrowed so much money from international banks and other countries that it has a huge national debt.

Eva Perón
Eva Perón (known as Evita) was born in the country but went to Buenos Aires and made her name as an actress. She married Juan Perón in 1945. Her popularity strengthened his position as president. She ran her own Social Aid Foundation for people in need, who adored her. Millions mourned when she died in 1952, only 33 years old.

The Falkland Islands
These islands have been a British colony since the beginning of the 19th century. They have a population of about 2,000, most of whom are sheep farmers. The islands are rough moorland and are off the coast of Argentina which has made many claims to own them. The Argentine name for the Falklands is Islas Malvinas. In 1982 Argentina invaded the islands, but were defeated by a British task force. This is the cathedral in Stanley, the capital of the islands.

Casa Rosada

The "Pink House," shown on the right, is the presidential palace where the president works.

"The Disappeared"

During the military rule of 1976-1983 it is thought that between 15,000 and 30,000 people were arrested, imprisoned, and murdered, some because they were suspected of being against the military rulers; others for no apparent reason at all. Many people are still trying to find out what happened to their relatives. The woman above holds up a picture of her daughter, one of "The Disappeared."

31

REPORTING THE NEWS

R adio and television provide important links between Buenos Aires and the rest of the country. They enable news to travel quickly over the vast distances, bringing the extreme north and south into daily contact. There are four main television channels in Buenos Aires. Argentinians like to watch sports and movies, many of which are imported from America and Europe. There are also educational and university channels and many provincial TV stations.

Today there is freedom of the press in Argentina, though it has been censored at different times in the past. President Perón closed down the country's oldest newspaper, *La Prensa*, which was founded in 1869, but it has since reopened. Other major daily papers in Buenos Aires include *La Nación, Clarín, Crónica,* and the financial paper *Ambito Financiero.* Each major provincial town also has its own newspaper. About 297 are published daily throughout the country.

An English newspaper
Buenos Aires has a daily newspaper published in English. *The Buenos Aires Herald* was founded in 1876 to cater to English-speaking immigrants. Today it has a circulation of about 20,000.

Family viewing
There are about 7 million television sets in Argentina. Many of these are owned by families who watch programs imported from abroad as well as those made in Argentina.

Selling the papers

Newsstands with Argentinian, Spanish, and a small range of other foreign magazines and newspapers are seen everywhere throughout the capital.

Jacobo Timerman

Jacobo Timerman created Argentina's first news magazine in the 1960s. Ten years later he published the first Argentinian newspaper to use up-to-date styles of journalism. It was called *La Opinión*. The paper was shut down by the military rulers of the late 1970s, and Timerman was expelled from Argentina.

ARGENTINIAN LIFESTYLES

Family life is important to Argentinians. Large families with several children are not unusual and different generations often live together. In low-income families both parents and children may work and grandparents help with the chores.

The lifestyle of an Argentinian family depends on where it lives and on its income. In the cities a family with a good income may live in one of the many apartment buildings or a comfortable house and own a car. Unemployed workers (some of whom come from the country seeking work) may live in sprawling shanty towns around Buenos Aires, often without electricity or running water. Families with low incomes may live in modest apartment buildings.

Families enjoy visiting relatives and often go on outings and also regularly attend church together. Teenagers and young people are expected to join in. Most young people live at home until they are married and many couples have to stay on in their parents' house because they cannot afford their own home.

Eating out
Families regularly eat out in restaurants and cafés and sometimes in the parks.

Suburban life
Houses in the suburbs of Buenos Aires or other cities are built of brick, wood, and stone. They are well designed to take advantage of sun and light. These houses have several bedrooms as well as quarters for a maid.

The Lottery
Lotteries are often held and most families can afford the price of a few tickets. The main prize can be a great deal of money or a car as in this lottery in Salta.

Mud brick houses
In country districts such as this one in northwest Argentina, houses are built of mud bricks. They are small, with only two or three rooms, basic furniture and a small cooking area. Many houses in remote locations have no electricity.

FOOD AND SHOPPING

Throughout Argentina restaurants and sidewalk cafés are extremely popular and serve a wide variety of good food. The favorite dish is grilled steak with potatoes and salad – often tomato and onion tossed with locally produced olive oil. Usually some beef is eaten daily even by people on low incomes.

The immigrant population of Argentina has introduced many different dishes such as pizzas and sausages. No Argentinian eats without wine. It is plentiful and inexpensive.

Shopping facilities of every kind are available in Argentina, from the sophisticated shopping arcades of Buenos Aires to country markets. Most towns have both supermarkets and traditional local shops. Clothes and other goods can be bought in boutiques which, in Buenos Aires, reach Parisian levels of sophistication. Window decoration has a flair and style unique in South America.

Snacks

An inexpensive snack is the *choripan*: fresh "French" bread and sliced, grilled *chorizo* – sausage spiced with pepper. Another snack is the *sandwich de miga* – coarse, crumbly bread and slices of ham and cheese. This sign is advertising a three-layered sandwich.

Fruits and vegetables

Vegetables and fruits are often sold from well-presented stalls, the prices clearly labeled according to the local law.

Harrods of South America
Once a branch of the famous London store, the Harrods in the center of Buenos Aires continues to reflect British tradition.

The pizzeria
Many Italians migrated to Argentina in the 19th century. One sector of Buenos Aires, La Boca (the mouth), is Italian. There you can eat Italian food and hear Italian spoken. There are estimated to be 2,000 pizza restaurants in the city. Here a pizza is being made in a restaurant kitchen.

LIFE ON THE RANCH

Until a few years ago a large ranch or estancia could cover an area of 400 square miles – about the size of Hong Kong. Most of the estancias in the Humid Pampas of the east have now been divided up. New machinery and more roads mean that fewer gauchos are needed to work on eastern estancias.

In the west, the estancias of the Dry Pampas are not so easy to farm with machinery. Here the gaucho is still vitally important.

Gauchos lead a hard life rounding up cattle through days of extreme heat and cold, and often of drought. Most of their work is done on horseback. They may spend days away from the estancia, sleeping out on the pampas, driving cattle to the slaughterhouse.

Part of the gauchos' job is to maintain gates, fences, and corrals in which cattle are kept. Gauchos also care for horses, many of which roam freely on the pampas. Most estancias have a ranch house where gauchos can sleep and eat. Their breakfast is a porridge of cornmeal and meat, with mate tea. Out on the pampas they live on barbecued meat.

Gaucho dress
The gaucho has been part of Argentine life for the last 400 years. Many fought bravely in the wars for independence. The wide, pleated trousers are called *bombachas*. They are tucked into high leather boots and held at the waist with a colored band. His *facón* – an extremely sharp knife in a leather case – is tucked into the band.

Festive barbecue
National holidays and festivals are celebrated with an *asado*, or barbecue, by the people of the estancia and their neighbors. Beef, mutton, and young goats are barbecued over charcoal fires in open pits. The meat is seasoned with a special sauce and sliced straight from the spit with the *facón*.

Southern estancia

The estancia shown on the right is in the far south of Patagonia, near Tierra del Fuego. Estancias in this region mainly rear sheep.

Out on the pampas

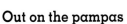

Gauchos herding cattle on an estancia in Entre Rios. The first cattle were brought by the Spanish in the 16th century. New breeds, including Hereford, Aberdeen Angus, and zebu have been introduced.

GOING TO SCHOOL

In Argentina all children between the ages of six and 14 have to go to school, by law. Free education is available for everyone. About 90 percent of the children go to school at some time, but many drop out because they are needed to work for the family, either on the land or to earn money in the cities.

There are state and private schools for primary and secondary level, and those in the cities are usually better equipped than those in the country areas. Schools are similar to those in the United States and classes include science, mathematics, languages, art, history, sports, and geography. Among Latin American countries, Argentina has a high level of education and literacy. Over 95 percent of the adult population can read and write.

Argentina has a strong university tradition. The oldest universities are Córdoba (1613), Buenos Aires (1812), and La Plata (1897). Today there are over 50 universities and more than half a million university students in Argentina.

Nobel Prize
Argentinian scientists who have won Nobel prizes include Bernardo Houssay in medicine (1947) and Luis F. Leloir (above) in chemistry (1970).

The school day
There are not enough state primary and secondary schools to teach all children at the same time. Pupils go to school either in the morning, or in the afternoon.

The oldest university

Córdoba University was the first to be founded in Argentina. In 1918 students at Córdoba went on strike until it was agreed that they should run the university jointly with the professors.

Domingo Faustino Sarmiento

President of Argentina from 1868-1874, Sarmiento was a great educationalist. He introduced primary education, founded free libraries throughout the country, brought in teachers from abroad, started school inspections, night school, and the teaching of physics and physical science. He built the first observatory in Argentina.

41

HAVING FUN

Argentinians are very keen on sports and their favorite game is soccer. Any small patch of ground is used to kick a ball around, and in Buenos Aires 17 soccer stadiums are packed with millions of spectators every weekend. The national team regularly participates in the World Cup, which Argentina has won twice.

With their traditional skill on horseback, Argentinians also excel at polo and show jumping, and their teams take part in many international events. During vacations and on the weekends, people like to go to the races, particularly in Buenos Aires where there is a fine racecourse that seats about 45,000 people. Outside the cities, there are good hunting and fishing areas, but the favorite sport for many is skiing.

The traditions of the various immigrant nationalities are still celebrated in festivals and fairs. Everyone enjoys Carnival which takes place in February or March. Many of the dancers taking part spend months preparing their costumes for the street parades.

Mar del Plata
Many Argentinians take their vacations at the popular resort of Mar del Plata, 250 miles from the capital. In the summer about two million visitors stay there. The city has a well-known casino and there are 5 miles of beaches.

Iguazú Falls

The Iguazú Falls on Argentina's border with Brazil and Paraguay are one of the most spectacular tourist attractions. Iguazú is a South American Indian word meaning "great waters." The falls are 8,100 feet wide, and an estimated 296,640 cubic feet of water per second crash down the 196 foot precipice.

Carnival time

At Carnival time in Buenos Aires there is a special night for children and the streets are filled with processions, musicians, and dancers. It is vacation time for everyone.

TOMORROW'S ARGENTINA

S ome Argentinians think that Argentina needs to make a new start. They believe that the country needs a chance to recover from debt – and to get rid of the old division between Buenos Aires and the rest of the country, making it more united. They believe that Argentina's future lies in Patagonia.

Patagonia has potential. Some of Argentina's largest oil and gas fields are there together with many unused mineral resources, there are large fruit growing areas and tourist regions, and the country's largest hydroelectric plants are nearby. All this is waiting to be developed.

As a first step towards developing Patagonia, President Alfonsín has suggested that the capital of Argentina be moved from Buenos Aires to Viedma, a small town in Patagonia. Government and business would be conducted from a new capital city. As yet, not many people are convinced that it will happen. Building a new capital would be very expensive and persuading people to live in Viedma may prove difficult, but there is growing opinion that Argentina must move into the 21st century with a new industrial and technological outlook. Perhaps Patagonia is the place to start.

President Raúl Alfonsín.

Black gold

Oil was discovered in Comodoro Rivadavia in 1907. Today there are over 6,000 wells and Comodoro Rivadavia has developed from a small settlement into one of the most important towns in Patagonia.

44

A changed landscape?
The sun sets on the remote and unspoiled landscape of the southern Andes. All this may change if future generations of Argentinians take up the challenge of Patagonia.

Tourist attraction
Calafate, a little town on Lake Argentino, and other towns like it, may benefit greatly if Patagonia is developed. It has a small tourist industry which could be expanded.

Index

Acknowledgments

All illustrations by Ann Savage.
Photographic credits (a = above, b = below, m = middle, l = left, r = right):
All photographs by Tony and Marion Morrison/South American Pictures,
except cover bl Robert Harding Picture Library; page 7 Stephen Pern/
Hutchison Library; page 10 W. Hasenberg/Zefa; page 11 b Hilary Bradt/ South
American Pictures; page 23 b Hilary Bradt/South American Pictures; page
38 Hilary Bradt/South American Pictures; page 39 a Robert Harding
Picture Library.